A Time We Knew

Books in the Basque Series

A Book of the Basques
by Rodney Gallop

In A Hundred Graves: A Basque Portrait
by Robert Laxalt

Basque Nationalism
by Stanley G. Payne

Amerikanuak: Basques in the New World
by William A. Douglass and Jon Bilbao

Beltran: Basque Sheepman of the
American West
by Beltran Paris, as told to William A. Douglass

The Basques: The Franco Years and Beyond
by Robert P. Clark

The Witches' Advocate: Basque Witchcraft
and the Spanish Inquisition (1609–1614)
by Gustav Henningsen

Navarra: The Durable Kingdom
by Rachel Bard

The Guernica Generation: Basque Refugee
Children of the Spanish Civil War
by Dorothy Legarreta

Basque Sheepherders of the American West
photographs by Richard H. Lane
text by William A. Douglass

A Cup of Tea in Pamplona
by Robert Laxalt

Sweet Promised Land
by Robert Laxalt

Traditional Basque Cooking History and
Preparation
by José María Busca Isusi

Basque Violence: Metaphor and Sacrament
by Joseba Zulaika

Basque-English Dictionary
by Gorka Aulestia

The Basque Hotel
by Robert Laxalt

Vizcaya on the Eve of Carlism: Politics and
Society, 1800–1833
by Renato Barahona

Contemporary Basque Fiction: An Anthology
introduction and commentary by Jesús María
Lasagabaster

English-Basque Dictionary
by Gorka Aulestia and Linda White

Negotiating with ETA: Obstacles to Peace in
the Basque Country, 1975–1988
by Robert P. Clark

A Time We Knew: Images of Yesterday in the
Basque Homeland
photographs by William Albert Allard
text by Robert Laxalt

The Basque Series

A Time We Knew

Images of Yesterday in the Basque Homeland

Photographs by William Albert Allard

Text by Robert Laxalt

University of Nevada Press   Reno & Las Vegas

Basque Series Editor: William A. Douglass

Publication of this book was made possible by generous grants from the John Ben Snow Trust and the E. L. Cord Foundation. Without their support the book could not have been published in its present form.

The paper used in this book meets the requirements of American National Standard for Information Sciences – Permanence of Paper for Printed Library Materials, ANSI Z39.48-1984. Binding materials were chosen for strength and durability.

Library of Congress Cataloging-in-Publication Data

Allard, William Albert.
    A time we knew : images of yesterday in the Basque homeland / photographs by William Albert Allard ; text by Robert Laxalt.
        p.   cm. — (Basque series)
    ISBN 0-87417-157-1 (alk. paper)
    1. País Vasco (Spain)—Description and travel.
    2. Pays Basque (France)—Description and travel.
    3. País Vasco (Spain)—Description and travel—Views. 4. Pays Basque (France)—Description and travel—Views.   I. Laxalt, Robert, 1923–
    II. Title.   III. Series.
    DP302.B46A4   1990
    946'.6—dc20   90-12259
                                                  CIP

Photo credits: The photographs on pages 12, 40, 53, 59, 61, 79, and 98 are used by permission of the National Geographic Society. Copyright 1968 by the National Geographic Society, Washington, D.C. Other photos © 1989, 1990, by William Albert Allard.

University of Nevada Press, Reno, Nevada 89557 USA
Copyright © University of Nevada Press 1990
All rights reserved
Designed by Richard Hendel
9 8 7 6 5 4 3 2 1

Printed in Japan

For my son, Anthony,
born twenty years after these photographs were made.
And for my wife, Ana Maria Baraybar Allard,
in whose veins flows the Spanish Basque blood of her ancestors.
  William Albert Allard

For my brothers John and Peter.
  Robert Laxalt

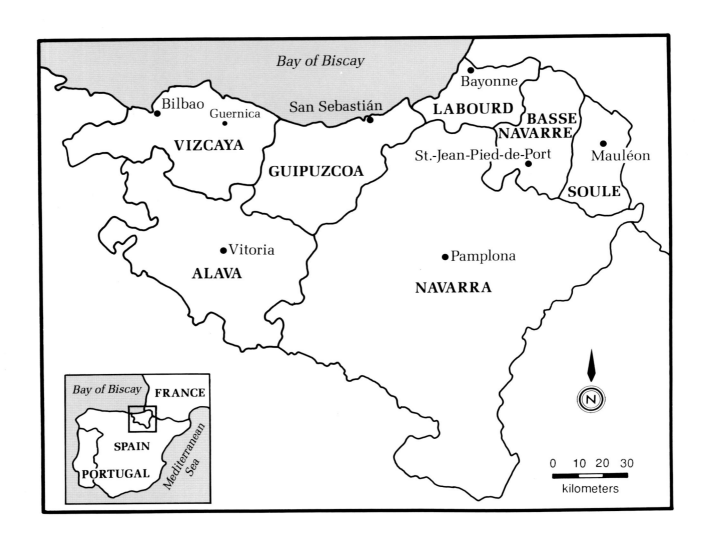

The Basque Country

Bay of Biscay

Bilbao
Guernica
San Sebastián
Bayonne
LABOURD
BASSE NAVARRE
VIZCAYA
GUIPUZCOA
St.-Jean-Pied-de-Port
Mauléon
SOULE

Vitoria
Pamplona
ALAVA
NAVARRA

Bay of Biscay
FRANCE
SPAIN
Mediterranean Sea
PORTUGAL

N

0 10 20 30
kilometers

About the Basques

The tiny homeland of the Basques – barely a hundred miles in diameter – straddles the crest of the western Pyrenees Mountains between France and Spain.

It is a land of deep oak forests, green mountain valleys, and the rugged sea-coasts of the Bay of Biscay.

In these mountains and on these shores dwell an ancient people called Basques. Where they come from, nobody knows. They probably wandered into the Pyrenees millennia ago, but some scholars claim they are the pure descendants of Cro-Magnon man, who evolved in an isolated setting here, fiercely resisting all invaders.

One thing is certain. The Basques are a distinct people who by blood and language are unrelated to the Indo-Europeans who dominated the rest of Europe.

The mystery of their origins has never been unlocked.

About the Book

During the decade of the 1960s, the seeds of change began to stir in the homeland of the Basques.

Before that, an old, old way of life had remained virtually unchanged in the villages and on remote farms, and living there was like being thrust a century backwards in time.

A photographer with rare talent came into the country one day and, understanding what he saw, preserved the vestiges of a peasant way of life before they were lost forever.

This book, then, is a chronicle of that time.

Robert Laxalt

About
the
Photographer

In the fall of 1967 I spent a little more than two months in the Basque country of Spain and France. Unlike my colleague, Robert Laxalt, Basque blood doesn't flow in my veins. And, unlike Bob, I never lived in the Basque country; I was merely a visitor. There's a lot I didn't see during my short stay – aspects of traditional Basque life that I couldn't photograph because I didn't witness them. The images in this book are the result of a short visit to a place that probably requires a lifetime to really know and maybe longer to truly understand.

I certainly didn't understand the language, more foreign to my not-very-well-traveled ears than I can now describe. But somehow, perhaps in the bliss of my ignorance, I guess I felt I didn't have to understand that strange Basque tongue. What was more important to me then was that I felt good there. I felt I was in the right place at the right time. And the place was beyond language.

Late one afternoon, with dusk coming on, I was driving down out of the mountains with my friend, Jean Garicoitz, to his home in St.-Jean-Pied-de-Port. The fading light became a hazy gray veil cast over the rugged landscape and all it contained. Shadows took the shape of objects and objects became shadows. "We have a saying for this time of day," Jean said. "Le temps entre chiens et loups," he said, in French. "The time between dogs and wolves." I have often thought of that phrase in the years since my brief stay among the Basques and how different that time was from the more recent years of bloodshed and tears that have fallen on both sides of the Basque country because of the brutal and deathly conflict of separatism.

On the night of the last day of September 1967, I celebrated my thirtieth birthday alone in a small cafe in St.-Jean-Pied-de-Port. I still remember that evening, not so much for any significance attached to having left the decade of my twenties, but for the memorable quiet solitude of the night, the clean, clear air of the mountains, and the feeling of being in the midst of a country and its people unlike any other in the world. I somehow felt in tune with the place. I loved it but couldn't quite say why. In retrospect, I suppose it was simply the right moment to be there. I was a young man in an ancient land. And it was the time between dogs and wolves.

William Albert Allard

A Time We Knew

In spring when the grass on the mountains has grown enough so that there is something of nourishment in it, the sheep move from the valley farms to the green slopes above the timberline.

Jean Pierre the shepherd had begun moving his flock in the darkness before dawn. When there was more light, we had followed after with the jeep and trailer.

The trailer was partitioned with boards. One side of the partition was filled with pink young pigs, each with a wire loop piercing its nose. This would make it too painful for the pig to root in the tiny garden beside Jean Pierre's stone hut. The other side of the partition was filled with provisions that Jean Pierre could not grow, such as coffee and sugar and spices. A wicker basket contained a substantial lunch of sardines and *paté de la maison,* ham and cheese and French bread, and a kidskin wine pouch that the Basques call *chahakoa.*

In the early morning, our village of St.-Jean-Pied-de-Port was still. We passed the stone ramparts that encircled the old fortified part of the village and wound up the sinuous dirt road that has been called Napoleon's route since the time of his occupation of the Basque provinces of France.

The route was flanked by berry bushes and roses and stone farmhouses with great wooden shutters thrown open to the fresh air of a new day. Farm women in black and gray aprons and straw hats, working in their gardens, stopped to watch the diversion.

When the road had climbed high enough, we could look down over a precipice and see the entire valley of the Cize – or Caesars, from the time of *their* occupation of the Basque regions.

The emerald green fields that surrounded our village and the hamlets were divided by hedgerows and stone fences. None of the fields were of the same shape, neither rectangular nor oval. Some of them were brown, newly tilled for the spring planting of corn.

Our village of St.-Jean-Pied-de-Port and the hamlets beyond were dominated by lofty church steeples. Whitewashed stone houses with red tile roofs surrounded these steeples like chicks around a mother hen.

We began passing little flocks of sheep, each animal with a distinguishing splash of red, green, or blue paint on its back so that it could be separated easily from other sheep if the flocks should mix.

The sheep are aristocratic in the Basque country, with graceful curling horns and patrician faces. Since they were leaving the warm valley for the cool nights of the high mountains, they still wore their wool so long that their fleeces seemed to touch the ground. When the summer was further along and the sheep grew accustomed to the cold, the shepherds would shear them.

The sound of bells filled the air — deep-sounding gongs of bells attached to wooden collars around the necks of the leaders, mellower sounding bells for the yearlings, and tinkling little bells for the lambs. Shaggy little sheepdogs with bobbed tails trotted like sentinels on the flanks of the flocks to keep them in proper place in the long procession.

The shepherds followed, knotted burlap and canvas sacks flung over a shoulder with lunch to be eaten along the trail. In case of rain, long black umbrellas were hooked by their handles to the back of the shepherds' coat collars. In their hands, the shepherds also carried slender whittled walking sticks called *maki-lak* in Basque. Donkeys followed after, borne down with provisions for the stone huts in which the shepherds would live until the coming of winter.

The shepherds were gruff, taciturn men with the unsmiling stamp of solitude on their faces. They were known as proper shepherds.

Not so Jean Pierre. Beneath the curling black hair that pushed out from under his beret, he had merry gray eyes and a shy but open smile. "I thought I might die of starvation before you caught up with me," he said to us.

"Do you want to eat now?" my cousin Chalbat asked.

"No. When the sheep stop for the noonday rest," Jean Pierre said. "At the shepherds' shrine, I think."

We went ahead and passed through the last of the forests below the timberline. It was a forest of beech and chestnut and great gnarled oaks whose foliage nearly blotted out the sun. The path was dappled with shadows the leaves made, and the moss and lichen on the great oaks was so thick that my probing fingers could sink into it like fur.

A wooden bridge with branches for handholds spanned a chasm, and here the sheep had to be herded across with much care. Below the wooden bridge, a cascade of water went flashing down over shining stones, making deep pools where the shadows of trout were like dark, barely moving phantoms. The sound of the swiftly moving water was a muted murmur.

And then suddenly, the forest ended and we were above the timberline. Vast sweeps of green mountains rose above us, broken only by outcroppings of white rock rearing from the carpet of grass. And I remembered what my father had told me in America of how, as a barefoot shepherd boy he would balance himself on his walking staff and glide down the long slopes with his *makila* hissing like a snake as it passed through the tender new grass.

The shepherds' shrine where we stopped to wait for Jean Pierre was above the timberline, too, atop a grassy knoll. There stood a bronze statue painted white of the Virgin Mary with a crown on her head and her arms holding the child Jesus with hands outstretched.

A spiral of steps had been cut into the sod for the priest, who on Ascension Day in May, said Mass there. Shepherds from all parts of the mountains would gather for the occasion. The huge rock that supported the statue was covered with shepherds' names cut into the surface to mark their visit.

Jean Pierre's sheep took their noonday rest in a depression of ground off the trail, so as not to mix with the passing caravan of flocks. After Jean Pierre had knelt at the shepherds' shrine to ask for protection for his sheep, his nephew helper, and himself, he climbed up to where we had spread the lunch.

His sheepdog stayed to guard the flock against a vulture who had taken too much interest in the lambs for Jean Pierre's liking. Frustrated, the vulture left for easier hunting, his black head jabbing forward from his brown body as he hopped awkwardly along the ground to get into flight. But there was nothing except gracefulness in his movements when he took to the air. His wings must have spanned six feet.

Except for Jean Pierre, who had been on the trail many hours and therefore had a big appetite, we munched our food slowly, washing it down with jets of red wine from the *chahakoa*. Afterwards, we lazed in the gentle spring sun and listened to Jean Pierre tell stories.

Not too far distant from us was a ravine carved through the ages by a spring bubbling out from under a jumble of white rocks. The spring's water coursed over pebbles and clear sand, forming deep and cold pools. Jean Pierre told of two French fishermen whom he had met once on the trail. They had asked him where good fishing was and Jean Pierre said to them, "Come, I will show you."

He led them to the largest of the pools. But when Jean Pierre saw myriad flitting shadows of trout, he told the Frenchmen. "I might as well catch some for my dinner, too."

The French fishermen looked at him with sly smiles, fingering their expensive equipment. "But you have no pole or lures or bait," they said.

Jean Pierre had said nothing. He rolled his pantlegs up to his knees, flipped off his sandals, and waded into the stream below the pool, so as not to disturb the Frenchmen's fishing. Bending over, he slipped his hands slowly into the icy water and kept them there until the trout had become accustomed to their presence.

When that time came, Jean Pierre began slowly to caress the trout's undersides. At first, the trout darted away but always they came back, liking the caress. When Jean Pierre's thumbs and forefingers were in position, he thrust them forward into the trout's gills, flipping the fish neatly onto the bank. In a few moments, he had caught thirty trout for his and his nephew's dinner.

When Jean Pierre strode whistling up the hill with his string of trout slung over a shoulder, he glanced back. The French fishermen were simply staring, their mouths agape.

Leaving Jean Pierre behind with his flock, my cousin and I climbed high above the timberline, where there were a hundred small hollows in the ground. In the sheltered lee of these hollows stood the stone huts which Basque shepherds and their barbarian ancestors had occupied from that long-ago day when they had ventured from their caves. We passed a dozen ruins of abandoned huts before we came to the rim above the stone hut that had been in Jean Pierre's family for generations uncounted.

The hut was built in a pyramid shape with thick walls made of big stones and little stones fitted together and chinked with clay. Hand-adzed oaken beams connected the sides and supported the heavy shingles of crudely shaped slate. The structure could have withstood a hurricane.

Abutting the cabin, there was an oval paddock for the sheep, made also of stones but with wooden crosspieces for gates. Twice a day, once at dawn and again at dusk, the sheep would be milked. Shuffling forward on their knees, Jean Pierre and his nephew would move through the sheep to gather milk for making the great round shepherds' cheeses that are a delicacy of the country.

The milk would be poured into small pails, and rennet added. When the cheeses began to form they would be transferred to circular molds made of long, pliable wooden laths that wound round on themselves and were secured by heavy cords. The cords would be tightened each day so that the thin fluid residue would trickle down onto a grooved wooden board and become skim milk for the shepherds' diets.

As we looked down from the rim, a wreath of blue smoke from the roof aperture told of the presence of Jean Pierre's nephew. With only a small sack of provisions to sustain him, the youth had hiked from the village to the hut several days before. His task had been to make the hut ready for occupancy by sweeping it out, building a big fire to consume the mustiness within, and warm the walls. He had also repaired the pig pen and the fence that would contain the garden, whose soil he had turned for planting. Here would grow carrots and cabbage and leeks to supplant their diet until autumn.

We called down from the rim to alert Jean Pierre's nephew of our presence. He emerged briefly, a lean youth with a shock of black hair. At this distance, he provoked an image within my mind of my father as a young man. But unlike my father, his reception was unsmiling almost to unfriendliness. He was already learning shepherd ways.

Leaving the jeep and the trailer at the rim, we carried the provisions down and deposited them on the stoop. The youth took them inside by himself, putting some in a sturdy wooden chest that would protect them from meadow mice, hanging the hams and bacons in their white cotton shrouds from the cross beams, and placing lamps and candles in hollowed out pockets in the stone walls. The tools he stacked in a corner.

All this we saw later after he had finally and reluctantly invited us inside. If he had had his way, we never would have entered.

Bending almost double, I went in through the low door. The hut was thick with gloom. A shaft of light came from the smokehole in the roof, another from a narrow slit cut into the stone walls. There was an open fire burning in a small pit with stones on its sides. A length of iron curved like a hairpin rested on the stones, and an aroma of coffee came from the blackened pot that rested on the fire iron. It was not unlike the sheepcamp arrangement with which I had grown up in the American West.

My cousin and I sat down on the wooden stools that flanked the fire and warmed our hands. The youth retreated to one of the two wooden beds with bracken-stuffed mattresses at the ends of the hut. In the firelight, I could see that he had a fine thin face and dark eyes.

When Jean Pierre arrived and had put the sheep into the paddock for the night, the youth went out with obvious relief to do his milking chores. My cousin and I had coffee laced with rum to warm us. But Jean Pierre, weary after a long day and an arduous climb, had pernod, that licorice-tasting liquor that turns milky when water is added. "This I permit myself only after I have earned my cup," he said, smiling. "I earn many cups in this life up here."

When we left the hut, Jean Pierre accompanied us to the rim despite all the walking he had done that day. Dusk was descending and the stone huts of the shepherds in their sheltered lees revealed themselves with glints of warm light. The youth did not even raise his head when we took our leave, but went on about his work.

He will make a proper shepherd, that one.

Behorleguy
France

Jean Baptiste
grandson of
Jean Mainhaguiet
Ibarrole
France

Jean Mainhaguiet
Ibarrole
France

Larrau

France

Mendive

11
France

Wedding party
St.-Jean-Pied-de-Port
France

12

Vespers
Ste.-Engrace
France

Sare

France

The Basque Country then was a land of song.

Rich tenor voices escaping from a bistro at night and reaching out to touch you as you walked down a village street. And inside another bistro, two men in berets with elbows planted staunchly on the table and a bottle of red wine between them, singing melancholy songs in baritone voices, lamenting times past and their lost youth. Their voices blending so closely that they were like one voice.

This was a land where only in song was one permitted to reveal true emotion. To talk about one's feelings then would have been a breach of dignity and stoicism.

Happiness, love, sorrow, melancholy, laughter – all were reserved for song. Basques had to clothe their sentiment and so preserve their privacy under a cloak of music.

Girls slender as reeds walking hand in hand down the lane, singing an ode to spring in soprano voices pure and light as air.

Boys going homeward to their farmhouses and their chores after school with arms entwined, diminishing in number one by one as they reached their homes. Singing of girls and sports and teachers. Finally, there is but one boy left. It does not matter. He sings alone at the top of his voice, making up for the loss of others.

A shepherd boy on a green slope above his home, imitating the notes of a flute as he trails his flock to its manger at dusk.

A peasant caught in silhouette against the skyline at end of day, his curved scythe resting on his shoulder like the specter of legend. He is singing an air without words, voicing in song his happiness with his world as he wends his way homeward to shelter, a warming fire, a good wife, and adoring children.

A Basque in his cups being told in a bistro that his uncle had died in California, and his response: "If there were any wine left in California my uncle would not have died."

A group of young men singing Basque songs at a bistro in Pamplona during the wine-drenched fiesta days of San Fermin. Because this was the time of Franco in Spain, the *Guardia Civil* came in and ordered them to stop. And one Basque youth said, "You may stop my Basque song, but you cannot stop my Basque heart."

The mariners' Mass at the fishing port of St.-Jean-de-Luz, with burly men's voices booming down with the sound of the deep sea in which they make their lives. They stand in the balconies that surround the nave, their scarred hands resting on railings oiled and worn smooth by two centuries of fishermen's hands. From below, the voices of wives and daughters sing the priest's part of the Mass, rising up in soprano counterpoint that pierces the booming like the piping of flutes.

But everyone who sings must defer to the bard, or *bertsolari* as he is known in Basque. He is the prince of song.

Once, the institution of the bard was a thing of all European peoples, from ancient Greece to Old England. It has been lost there, but like so many mysteries, it has managed to live on in this land of antiquity.

The Gascons of Cyrano were excellent bards worthy of meeting in contest, the Basques say, but they also say that the phenomenon of the Basque *bertsolari* is older and therefore better.

A youth begins his career as a bard in the Basque Country when those who know best have remarked on his richness of voice and magic with words. Then he is encouraged to go on, singing at weddings and village feasts and finally in contest with other *bertsolariak*.

Each develops his forte, be it droll or melancholy, passionate or acerbic in satire. If he is a sailor he will be called upon to praise the merits of a shepherd's life, and vice versa. If he is a bachelor, he will be called upon to sing the praises of a married man's life. If he has chosen to stay in the Basque Country instead of emigrating to the Americas, he will be called upon to praise the life of a stranger in foreign parts.

Once, I heard a bard sing a story of a Basque who had sold his soul to the devil in exchange for money. With one condition. When the devil came to claim his soul at the end of his life, the Basque would be permitted to take his flute, his *chirula* or *txistu*, to Hell with him. The Basque in time died and went to Hell. When he got there, he began to play his flute. The furnace stokers threw aside their shovels and began to dance. So Satan had no choice but to kick the Basque out of Hell. None have gone there since.

Another time, in a bistro in the high mountains where my father was born, a *bertsolari* was asked to sing to me of Etchahun, his grandfather and the most famous of all the Basque bards who ever lived.

With absolutely no self-consciousness, the grandson of Etchahun sang to me. He related in song how Etchahun had shot his best friend at night, mistaking him for the suitor of his sweetheart's affections. With his friend's blood still on his hands, Etchahun fled to the high mountains and through tears sang of what he had done.

The shepherd boys who heard him sang long afterwards of Etchahun's tragedy, and finally the song made its way down to the valleys and the villages. It was still being sung in my time there.

But his grandson sang of what had not been told in Etchahun's agonized lament to the shepherd boys, the lament intact that has managed to live on. Etchahun had surrendered himself to the authorities and was sent to prison. When his time in prison was done, he imposed a special penance upon himself and walked to Rome and back.

When he died in old age, his possessions were burned at the nearest cross-roads, his clothing and bedding and all things of material value. That was the Basque custom in Etchahun's time, and it is understandable to me.

What is not understandable to me even now is that all of Etchahun's written verse was also heaped upon the pyre at the crossroads, to be consumed forever by the flames.

Perhaps the answer lies in an interlude I had with a monk at a Benedictine Monastery in the Basque Country. I asked the monk, whose business it was to know, how the Basques regarded writing in the scale of art.

The monk told me that singing, story telling in song, and dance were the highest forms of art. He could not bring himself to say where writing was ranked.

Marie Jose Lerissa
Behorleguy
19   *France*

A game of mus
Elorrio

Spain

Jota
Elorrio
Spain

Church balcony
Ste.-Engrace
France

Anne Marie Lerissa
Behorleguy
France

The coast near
San Sebastián

Spain

The echoes of the cannon's blasting roar rolled down the narrow cobblestone streets of the fishing village, bounding off the stone walls of houses and shops, rounding corners and thundering down other streets, seeking even the alleyways until every nook and cranny had been forewarned.

In a hundred tiny houses, fishermen at table leaped to their feet, their eyes alight with the expectation of adventure and foreign lands and modest fortune. Vanished in an instant was the frustration of a storm that had held the fishing fleet captive in the harbor.

For days, the heavy seas had come in from the great ocean beyond. The concrete barriers of the breakwater had broken the strength of the incredible waves, but there had been enough left to wash over the breakwater and pound the sea walls of the village so that it seemed even the stone houses shook endlessly.

For the wives of the fishermen, the cannon's roar was like the call of doom, bringing instant fear into their faces. They understood full well its meaning. Five months of winter in a village without men. Five months of bearing alone the responsibility of house and family and survival on meager fare until their husbands returned with purses filled with money. Children squealed with excitement, but in the corners by the fireplaces, grandmothers and widows in long black dresses lowered their knitting needles and made the sign of the cross. The cannon's roar held nothing new for them.

In less than an hour, it seemed as if everyone in the village was thronged on the quay bordering the harbor. Word had spread like wildfire that the open sea beyond was clear of storms. The captains of the fishing fleet had made a decision to chance a dash from the storm-locked harbor. The prize they pursued was the big schools of tuna that in winter migrate to the waters off Africa's western coasts. If the fleet waited any longer, the prize catches would be gone to competing fleets from Spanish ports.

The Basques have always gone to sea. The scene I was witnessing must not have been unlike another day many centuries before. Then, the signal tower overlooking the ocean had blazed and smoked with burning straw, announcing that a school of spouting whales had been sighted. From a dozen seacoast villages on the Bay of Biscay, the ancestors of these same sailors had put out to sea in caravels and pinnaces that the Vikings had taught them to build in the ninth and tenth centuries, when they put into Basque ports to recuperate from battle and mend their ships. But the quarry of the Basques then was far more dangerous than tuna.

Those early Basques were almost certainly Europe's first whalers, pursuing the leviathans of the deep up the coasts of Scotland and Iceland as far north as Spitzbergen, and across the uncharted Atlantic to Newfoundland, Labrador, and the mouth of the St. Lawrence River. Though they were unaware of the import of their feat, they may have visited the New World a century before Columbus, leaving behind them traces of their colonies and whaling trade.

The quay seethed with the emotions of farewell. Young mothers had brought their babies to watch husbands and fathers go to sea. Sweethearts in trim modern dresses waved to their young men busy in the boats that filled the little harbor, youths with sturdy frames and ruddy skin in sailors' garb — thick blue sweatshirts and turtlenecks, yellow oilskin pant coverings, and knit caps upon their heads.

The grandmothers had come too, to stand like apparitions in black coats, dark scarves covering their white hair, heavy shoes on their feet. Sailors too old to go lingered in the background. So did those bent by work or blinded in one eye by flying fishhooks, the blind eye covered with a black patch. A sailor who had lost an arm, standing apart, sang to his comrade on a boat, "I would rather have you back alive than be given a million dollars."

The boats made ready to go. One was the *Aigle des Mers*, the *Eagle of the Seas*, which I knew well. Its captain's quarters and shining navigation deck, its trim little galley for cooking, its little hatches filled to the brim with sardines as bait for tuna, and below decks, a cabin where fishermen's bunks were interlocked in a circle.

With pennants and streamers fluttering bravely, the blue and red and green painted boats left the quay in prearranged order. There were twenty-four boats in all, and they were to make the dash past the breakwater in groups of four. Dusk was coming on and the little boats looked like helpless waifs against the skyscrapers of water that crashed against the breakwater. They did not seem able to survive the rolling, thundering might of the sea.

But survive they did. And go they did, pitching and plunging and clinging together for protection. Twenty-four boats in groups of four, with lights blinking on as they made their swift dash to the safety of the open sea.

By the time the last blinking light had been lost to the black horizon, only one man was left on the quay. He was an old sailor whose voyaging days were done, and all that was left to him were memories of the blue seas and white sands of Africa, the glistening flanks of giant tuna as they were hauled over the rail to flop their lives out on decks slippery as ice, and finally the night of leave-taking in the bars of exotic Dakar before the boats made their homeward way laden down with booty from their eternal provider, the sea.

Pelota
St.-Jean-le-Vieux
France

Guernica
Spain

34

Workmen
Bacaicoa
Spain

Santesteban

Spain

San Sebastián

37

Spain

Spectators

Lesaca

Spain

San Sebastián

Spain

San Sebastián
Spain

Young hopefuls
San Sebastián
Spain

Weightlifting contest
San Sebastián
Spain

M arket day had been held in our village of St.-Jean-Pied-de-Port since memory began. I assume that is because St.-Jean is the largest, most centrally situated, and the oldest village in the province of Basse-Navarre. The fact that it is the oldest is important.

Market day did not mean commerce alone. It was business and pleasure, sport and song, courting and dancing intertwined leisurely one with another.

All roads and paths from hamlets and farms seemed to converge upon our village on the weekly market day. The lanes were lined with farmers leading or driving mule-drawn carts filled with animals bedded down on clean golden straw. Invariably, the mules were clipped halfway down their bodies so that their undersides were fringed with long hair.

If a farmer was a *petit paysan* and could not afford a cart, he would walk with his veal calves, one hand on a sturdy rope encircling the calf's neck and the other twisting the calf's tail so that it would behave.

Morning was the men's market and it was filled with the tumult of bawling calves, squealing pigs, and bleating lambs. The animals were led to pens and hitching posts next to the lichen-covered ramparts built in Napoleon's time to fortify the village.

The calves occupied one section designated by tradition and family use over the centuries, the sheep occupied another, and the pigs — some of them monstrous in size — were held captive in sturdy wooden pens. A loose pig maddened by noise and fear can create much havoc. Calves and sheep are more mildly disposed.

The animals made up a medley of muted colors — pigs pink and pigs mottled in pink and black, sheep with white curling wool, and calves dun, brindle, and tan.

The morning was given over to barter in the old way. Buyers from the coastal cities such as Bayonne, Biarritz, and St.-Jean-de-Luz arrived in big trucks. They wore long gray smocks with a pocket full of pencils, although I never saw a buyer use a pencil. The bartering was a pantomime done with gestures, contemptuous scowls, and indifferent shrugs, and finally the three hand slaps that sealed a transaction.

Give or take a few centimes, a lamb weighing twenty pounds would sell for 50 new francs — 10 dollars — and a veal for 500 new francs — 100 dollars. Because the buyers could sense how poor a peasant was, and they were all more or less poor, the seller would earn only enough to keep his family in clothes and footwear, his animals in medicine, and himself in tobacco.

When the men's market was done at midday, there was a lull. Farmers who could afford it gathered in the little restaurants for lunch and better wine than they were used to at home, and afterwards, if a sale had been unexpectedly rewarding, singing with old friends.

The farmers did not remove their berets when they ate, so that the restaurants become a sea of black berets, black broadcloth suits, and white shirts without neckties, because the Basques abhorred constriction.

If a *petit paysan* was too poor to eat lunch in a restaurant, he would find a spot of sun near the rampart, lean back against the old stone, and take his lunch of bread and cheese and wine from the cloth sack he had slung over his shoulder on leaving his farm.

It was during the lunch hour that mothers and old grandmothers and children took over the lanes that led from their farms to the village, carrying expansive baskets filled with vegetables to sell at market. The baskets also contained eggs placed in a pot filled with oats to keep them from breaking. Grandmothers were dressed in black, mothers in print dresses, and children in smocks to protect better clothes underneath from the ravages of wrestling matches, races, and handball games. Every flat wall in the village, including the church, would serve as a handball court of instant improvisation.

The afternoon was the women's market, and the main street and village square were lined with gaily colored awnings suspended over stalls in case of rain and long tables where farm women sold their vegetables and eggs. The stalls offered everything from needles and new kinds of thread to bolts of cloth and factory-made dresses.

The village women would wander from table to stall, making little purchases of fresh eggs and vegetables from the farm women and things such as head scarves from the transient *gitanes* who owned the stalls.

When the farm women had sold their products, they too would join the shopping others, but their purchases would always be small, and practical. But village women and farm women had known each other forever in this region of few people, so there was pleasure in stopping to visit and exchange gossip from town and country.

As shadows lengthened, the time of courting would begin. It was shy and distant courtship at best, with boys walking in groups with other boys, and girls with girls in groups that lingered calculatingly on the village square.

They would stop and talk as if meetings were by chance, but of course they were not. Even witn such infrequent encounters, romances were born.

When dusk began to fall, the time for dancing and sports had come. The village square was filled with twirling figures of the young dancing the *jota* or the more intimate but no less animated courting dance, the *auresku*. The notes of flute and accordion filled the air, and sometimes in the impromptu intermissions, a youth with a golden voice would sing a song that had been handed down to him in this land of oral tradition.

Inside the *trinquet,* the indoor handball court, the best of the players from the region would meet in contest. The games were pleasant affairs, but they were almost masochistic in the suffering they caused. The ball was hard and covered with doghide, and few were the champions whose fingers were not twisted and mangled by the force with which they struck the *pelota*.

The open-air fronton was more to my liking. It was situated in an amphitheater that resembled an arena from Roman times, complete with tiered banks of stone seats. The players were clad in white with red or green sashes around their waists, and their hands were attached to long, curved *chisterak* made of wicker. The required movements were graceful, the white ball soared into the night sky, and the score was counted out in a Basque chant that carried for half a mile.

When midnight came, the village streets were deserted and the lights in the bistros and restaurants blinked out one by one. The village folk had gone to bed.

The country folk had longer to go before they reached their farms. The lanes were lined with weary figures trudging homeward, and the carts were filled with children who had succumbed to sleep. They lay cuddled on the same straw that had bedded the animals on their way to market that morning.

The country folk faced tomorrow's chores with the prospect of dragging feet. But their hearts would be lighter, because there had been market day to savor.

St.-Jean-Pied-de-Port

France

Market day
St.-Jean-Pied-de-Port

France

Market day
St.-Jean-Pied-de-Port
France

Market day
St.-Jean-Pied-de-Port
France

Market day
St.-Jean-Pied-de-Port
France

Bermeo
Spain

52

Ezcurra

Spain

Sare

France

"Her second baptism," said my cousin Josef, his long thin face and blue eyes troubled. "Do you remember the old woman you met who was to have her second baptism today?"

I did remember her, but not the exact day on which she would be one hundred years old. She had a cavernous voice that rumbled up from a deep chest underneath her long black widow's weeds. Her hands were bent with work in the soil, but her black hair had only a touch of gray in it. Her face was remarkably unlined. One would have expected this in a younger woman who had spent her years in these pure mountains, but she would be one hundred years old in a few weeks.

"I took a detour to stop at her farm on my climb back up the mountain from the village," said Josef. "I was going to wish her happy century from our family."

Just after daybreak, Josef had had to clamber down to the village on the valley floor far below for coffee, sugar, and spices and things that could not be raised on his farm. It was no small undertaking. Josef's farm perched in a saddle of land very near the peak of the mountain. There were no roads to it, and the climb down to the village and back was almost a day-long ordeal.

Josef's house was a very old house on my father's side of the family. It was in the high mountains of the Pyrenees, and the Basques who lived in these forbidding mountains seemed like a race all their own. There were strange customs in this country.

The stone lintel above the door was carved with the date 1700, and the inset wooden braces in the whitewashed stone were so old that they were crumbling even though they were of oak. The yard around the house was muddy in winter when the snows melted, and pigs grunted and rooted there. The stable for the animals was joined to the house by a common wall, so that the heat from their bodies would keep the dining room warm.

In the front room, there was a black cave of a fireplace with heavy black chains hanging down for pots and cooking pans. Josef's old grandmother sat by the fire on her *amatchi*'s bench, sipping her soup. She was eighty-seven years old and still working in the vegetable garden. Once each week, she would carry the household laundry down to the creek a quarter mile below, wash it there in the icy water, and bring it back up to the house before nightfall. She had decided to live until she was ninety and no more.

I had known Josef was troubled when he strode through the wooden gate to the door. He stepped out of his wooden shoes and into his rope sandals before dropping his pack to the floor. He said nothing when we sat down together at the scarred oaken table in what went for a dining room. His wife, a square, solid woman with a round, ruddy face and pleasant eyes, served him soup. When he had nearly finished, he poured wine into his bowl, swished it around, and drank from it like a cup. Josef needed that for strength after the climb and whatever had happened to him at the century-old woman's farm.

When Josef and I had visited her there, the old woman had told us of hearing unexplained noises in her house at night. She was not exaggerating, because her family had heard them, too. They had decided that the noises were made by the *laminak,* the little people of Basque superstition who live in the deep forests.

"After we talked to her," said Josef, "the noises grew louder and every morning the family found something broken. So it was decided that the old woman must talk with the priest, who knows about these things."

Josef said that the old woman, despite her ninety-nine years, had climbed down to the village to see the priest. When my expression revealed disbelief, Josef shrugged. "That descent to the village is nothing," he said. Gesturing with his head to his grandmother sitting by the fireplace in the other room, Josef said, "*Amatchi* has done it many times."

Josef went on. "The priest told the old woman that the noises would persist until she made a pilgrimage on foot from her farm to the Chapel of the Madeleine. That meant that she must make the descent to the valley floor, walk to its end, and climb to the chapel that was situated on the very peak of the highest mountain in the range. Before Christian times, it had been a pagan shrine to the deity guarding the valley, the Goddess of the Red Dust. When the Romans came, they inscribed a slab at the foot of the shrine in respect to the Basque goddess. My wife and I had climbed that mountain once, and we were not anywhere near a hundred years old and we had been tired to death.

"The old woman made the pilgrimage," Josef said. "As the priest predicted, the night noises stopped."

"Well, what has gone wrong?"

"The old woman's son told me the priest had come up to the farm a few days ago."

"To verify that the night noises had stopped?"

"No," said Josef. "To remind the old woman that on her hundredth birthday, she must be baptized again."

I could not conceal my incredulity.

"It is the custom here in these mountains," said Josef defensively.

Then I asked what I did not want to ask. "Was she baptized again?"

Josef shook his head. "She hung herself this morning. In the stable."

"That is horrible!"

"No, it is not," said Josef firmly. "If you were wearing a hundred-year-old body, would you want to be born again by a second baptism?"

I had no answer to that.

"She couldn't endure the idea," Josef said. "She made up her mind yesterday that she would not be baptized again. The family accepted her decision."

"Then why did she kill herself."

"Because the *laminak* visited the house again last night. The noises have come back. Perhaps now that she has hung herself, the noises will go away again."

I listened to the fire whispering in the grate in the other room and thought of my grandaunt sitting by the fireplace. And remembered that she had vowed to live until she was ninety years old. And no more.

St.-Jean-de-Luz
France

Jai alai
Sare
France

Listening to a bertsolari
Sare

France

Monday market
St.-Jean-Pied-de-Port
France

I remember the first time I saw the oxen. I had come into the Basque Country at night, when the villages were locked in sleep. I stayed at a country inn with sweet smelling oaken floors rubbed down with beeswax and slept in a feather bed.

I had awakened in the morning to birdsong. Then I heard a sound I had never heard before. It was a great rumbling in the country lane that passed beside the inn. I leaped out of bed and threw open the big wooden shutters and looked down.

There, unbelievably, were two oxen pulling an old, creaking cart with wooden wheels nearly as tall as a man. There was a hand-hewn yoke resting on their necks just behind wide, curved horns wrapped at their bases with leather. Fringes made of red and green cording hung over their eyes, for what reason I could not determine.

The oxen were dun colored and huge, with cloven hooves that plodded in unison, just as their heads nodded in unison from their rhythmic stepping.

A Basque peasant with a black beret, worn blue cotton shirt, loose trousers, and wooden shoes that were filled with straw for stockings walked beside the oxen. He had a whittled wooden goad in his hand.

When the man and the oxen reached the crossroads, the peasant laid the goad flat over the oxen's necks and they stopped to let a car go by. The peasant raised the goad and the oxen resumed their pulling. In a little while, they had disappeared down the lane leading to the fields.

After that time, I got to know the ways of oxen well. I worked with them in the fields with my cousin, scattering fertilizer over the fields before planting corn, loading the carts with new-mown hay and hauling it to the lofty barn.

I learned that the fringe flapping over their eyes was not for decoration, but to keep the flies away, that the bases of their horns were wrapped with leather so that the yoke would not bruise their horns, that when the yoke is removed the belled collar, whittled from green willow, was put back around their necks.

In times before, the oxen were nearly always males, but now they had been replaced by females. In this way, the oxen served the double purpose of work and giving milk for butter and cheese.

I learned to love the oxen for their docility and patience. They were started in their training when they were four years old, and the first time in yoke, they accepted the burden and rarely caused trouble. Tired as they were after a long day's work, they never complained and they never faltered.

But I learned to love them for something more. Like their masters, they worked with a willing heart and needed no goading.

Monday market
St.-Jean-Pied-de-Port
France

Ram fighting
San Sebastián
Spain

After the fight
San Sebastián
Spain

67

Jean Mainhaguiet
with wife Gratianne
and son Pierre
Ibarrole
France

Txistu players
Sare
France

Bacaicoa
Spain

Pamplona

Spain

Corpus Christi feast day
Elorrio
Spain

Ibarrole

74   *France*

Once in our exploring, we took a road that went nowhere. It ran right into a mountain that was the frontier between France and Spain, and stopped. It ended where it did, definitely.

On the way up to the high mountains, we had followed a traveled road that flanked a swiftly descending river of shining white water that burst into rainbow-hued sprays when it struck the big rocks jutting from the riverbed.

This was a canyon and a region that few if any tourists had ever penetrated. This was a *coin perdu,* a lost corner in which Basque life had changed but little over centuries.

It was also the most beautiful countryside that I had ever seen anywhere.

Across the river, we saw little farms consisting of whitewashed stone houses and barns and vegetable gardens, and sometimes a vineyard. On the impossibly steep slopes around the farms, grazing sheep as small as puffs of white cotton seemed to cling tenaciously to the green mountain to keep from falling over.

There was a crude wooden bridge that spanned the river as a connecting link between the farms and the nearest village, Aldudes. It was a walking bridge, but at this time of day, it was patrolled by a white duck.

He waddled imperiously from one end of the bridge to the other. Once, when a boy not much older than ten attempted to step foot onto the bridge, the white duck flew at him in a rage. The boy retreated and returned a few minutes later with his mother wielding a broom. She chased the duck off the bridge, and the boy crossed on his errand to the village.

When we asked at the village beyond, the people said they found it amusing that the duck had taken possession of the passage. They had even named him the *patron* of the bridge, which is to say *master.*

The restaurant in which we had a long lunch was in the old manner. It contained only four small tables. In a corner, there was a crockery wash bowl with homemade soap and a common towel hanging from a peg. The window and the mirror on the wall were almost opaque from cooking and tobacco smoke. This was a Basque restaurant whose offerings and menu had not changed in a century. Already, its like had begun to disappear.

Our lunch began with an aperitif of Spanish sherry, followed by a tureen of vermicelli soup with thyme. It was fragrant and tasteful beyond belief. The trout that followed had been taken from the fish pen in the river after we had placed our order. It was sautéed in oil and garlic and sprinkled with parsley. The chicken entrée was roasted with olive oil and butter and it seemed to melt in my mouth. Then there was a salad of fresh lettuce and a secret house dressing. The wine was white and of the region, made from the grapes in the tiny vineyards we had seen along the way. Dessert was shepherd's cheese and French bread, and our repast was complete.

There were three men, not young, at one of the other tables. We fell into conversation with them and they began to tell about an incident that had happened in the village that past summer. In a lost village where little of importance ever happens, it was a puzzling and yet warming thing to watch their excitement as the story unfolded.

It seemed that a grand champion of handball, or *pelota,* was to come across the frontier from Spain and meet in contest with the champion of the village, who was not young but full of wiles gained through experience.

"The champion from Spain was denied entry at the frontier because his papers were not in order," the spokesman of the three old men said. "But the champion came anyway, taking a secret path through the forest. The match was played remarkably well, despite the fact that a French gendarme was waiting to arrest the champion from Spain when the match was done."

"Why didn't he arrest the champion right away?" I asked.

The old man's companion shook his head slowly. "That would have been an offense against all tradition," he said. "Just like Mass in church, a handball game must be completed."

"Did the gendarme arrest the champion?" I asked, knowing that I was obliged to.

The spokesman resumed his story. "The champion from Spain won the match," he said. "Which was expected because he was young. What was not expected was that as the gendarme approached, the champion threw the *pelota* at him. It was very hard and covered with doghide, as you know. The ball struck the gendarme in the head and knocked him unconscious. The champion from Spain fled into the forest and made his escape. That escapade was as rememberable as the handball match itself." The story teller was complacent and satisfied with his telling, and he beamed proudly when it was done.

We thanked the three men for the story and went to the kitchen to pay our bill and our respects to the *patron,* who was also the chef.

When the *patron* learned that my wife, Joyce, and I were American, he confided that he had sent his three sons to the United States from the little profit he made in the restaurant.

That revelation gave us a clue to something that had puzzled us. In our walk through the village, we had seen only very young children and men and women not at all young. There seemed to be nobody in-between.

Just outside the village, we found the road that went nowhere. It branched off the traveled road and was only wide enough for one car. Once on the way, we did meet another car and were forced to back up and teeter on the brink of the road as the descending car inched past us.

The countryside here was even more beautiful than below. It was wild and thick with birch and oak and rusted plum trees, close-growing clumps like flowering mounds all joined together, tipping over hills and descending the slopes. The forests were divided from the green pastures very distinctly by curved clean lines of green, pressed against the trees.

We came at last to the end of the road. It ran indeed into the base of the mountain and stopped there as if it had run into a stone wall. It was a curious end to a road.

For some reason unexplainable to me then, there was a combined house and restaurant at the end of the road. Outside, there was a terrace of slates and vines wound through a trellis overhead. We decided to stop for coffee.

The *patron* here was a big man with a deep chest and flaring gray mustaches. The end of the road was intriguing me more and more, and I asked the *patron* why it ended where it did.

He shrugged. "No more money," he said. "This is a poor country."

I asked him if there were tourists brave enough to venture into this lost corner for a meal. He answered that his lunch and dinner business was practically all from the handful of farm families tucked away in the mountains. They came for lunch on Sundays and feast days, weddings and first communions.

He confided too that he and his wife had sent their sons to America. In their case, four of them. "With the money they have sent back, we built this little restaurant," he said. "But even then, we would starve to death from what we earn here."

I was reluctant to ask the question, but he answered it without my having to. "See those mules down there," he said, pointing toward a wooden corral below that held six sturdy animals. "Those are Spanish mules. That is how I supplement our living. I am a *contrabandier*."

There was such obvious pride in his voice that we could not condemn him, even with our eyes. But he understood anyway, because when I said, gazing down the way we had come, "It's such a beautiful country," he nodded in agreement and said, "Yes, it's beautiful. But one cannot eat beauty."

Behorleguy
France

Lecumberry

France

Jean Pierre Bidonde
St.-Jean-Pied-de-Port
France

Bacaicoa

Spain

Ox shoeing
St.-Jean-Pied-de-Port

France

Dove hunt
Behorleguy
84   *France*

The sound of the distant horn came fluting up the brackened slopes. In the half light of the rude tree hut, the Basque hunter held up his hand for silence. The sound of the horn came again and this time the note of warning in it was unmistakable.

"So now it begins," he said. "You had better go down."

Three of us were cramped into the tower of death, a tiny tree hut perched in the topmost branches of a giant oak. The floor we stood on was piled with whittled wooden projectiles shaped like small paddles. Far beneath us in this high mountain path was an old stone cabin with a sagging roof whose slates were green with lichen. And beyond the cabin, strung on poles that towered 50 feet into the air, hung a sweep of nets so fine as to be almost invisible.

The *palombière,* a place for hunting doves, was one of a dozen situated in the high mountain passes of the Pyrenees. Here, for many hundreds of years the Basques have netted the wild dove in its autumn migration from Scandinavia to the warmer climes of Spain and Africa.

My cousin Petain and I descended the dizzying ladder from the tree hut to the ground. The villagers in the old stone cabin were scrambling out to dive into camouflaged mounds that held the levers to trip the great nets, others to conceal themselves behind a wooden barricade.

Through the eye slit in the barricade, I saw a flight of doves – dark specks in a broken arc – rising swiftly into the funnel of the pass. When they were so near that I could hear the drumming of their wings, the white wooden projectiles lanced out of the tower of death like falcons whirling down in attack.

The flight reared up like a single thing, and then, to protect itself, dived close to the ground and came the rest of the way to the nets in a blur of swiftness. When it struck the nets, there was a soundless explosion of feathers. Doves hung in awkward disarray in the webbed strands as though they had been pasted against a canvas sky.

Then the levers were jerked and the nets came tumbling down. The air was rent with a spine chilling Basque cry, and the villagers descended upon their catch.

Afterward, my cousin and I went down the mountain, walking under a crimson and gold canopy of beech and chestnut trees in full autumn color.

"Do you find it cruel?" my cousin asked.

"I don't think so," I said. "I thought it was old and beautiful in some strange way. But it was also tragic."

"We are not without feeling about the hunt of the doves," my cousin said. "There is even an old, old song about it that some say goes back to the time of the Romans."

"*Urzo chouria, urzo chouria . . .*" he began.
"White dove, white dove,
Tell me if you please:
Where were you traveling,
Your flight so straight,
Your heart at ease?"

"From my northern country I flew,
With the thought of seeing Spain.
I got as far as the land of the Basques,
There lost my pleasures,
And found pain."

Dove hunt
Behorleguy
France

Nicolas Lerissa
and grape harvest
Behorleguy
France

Antoine and
Nicolas Lerissa
Behorleguy
France

Loading hay
Lecumberry
90   *France*

Separating sheep
Larrau
France

The pilgrimage had begun at dawn, and the narrow path to the stone chapel wound up the mountain for ten miles.

The young walked in front, and the old behind, black-scarved grandmothers with twisted canes in their hands. The clouds hung in wreaths across the face of the mountain, so that sometimes those in the rear of the procession could not see the head of it.

The chapel was hidden in a depression on the crest of the mountain. Once, Basque warriors had hidden and sheltered here so that they could not be surprised by invading Germanic tribes; instead, they could launch their own assaults through the tangled forests below. In a later time, pilgrims on their tortuous road to Compostela had lingered here for rest and for protection from storms and Basque brigands.

The back of the stone chapel rested against the mountain, so that the upper level where the men entered was even with the ground. In front, the ground sloped away so that the women's entrance was level with the altar.

The door above and the door below were arched and narrow, so as to keep what warmth there was inside the chapel. The stone steps that led to both doors were worn down in the middle, which was natural after a thousand years of footsteps.

Inside the church, there were benches barely six inches wide with upright poles on the ends. They were axe hewn in a crude way, so that the marks still showed after centuries. There were no kneeling planks for the men in the gallery level above, so they stood during the consecration.

I had joined the men above. We looked down on an altar the likes of which I had never seen. It was a hand-painted altar with a blue background. Shepherds' symbols and crude drawings I could not decipher were painted upon the blue. Suspended above the altar was a gilded wooden sun with spreading rays so primitively painted they seemed to glimmer from another time. As indeed they did. I sensed it then, with shivers running up my spine, and learned it later. The altar had been a pagan shrine before the coming of Christianity.

The Basques do not like the physical presence of others pressed too closely to them, so it was the first time I had had a chance to see them in such proximity. The old man next to me was obviously a shepherd, not only from his tanned face but from the porcelain peace that rested lightly on his fine features. The Basque next to him could have stepped out of barbarian forests. His black eyes looked out fiercely from under jutting brows, and the force of his character emanated from him like a physical flow.

All of the men in the upper gallery were hunched on the thin benches with their elbows planted on their knees. They were dark-garbed with brown coats and blue wool pants, or black coats and brown pants, and uniformly black shoes with thick, sturdy soles. One Basque with shining gray hair and florid face and a red beaked nose wore a blue cotton smock and pantaloons and wooden shoes that he took off during the Mass. His bare feet were calloused and resembled wood.

Because it had rained that morning, the upper level was suffused with the smell of wet wool and clean sweat of men whose bodies were purified by work.

The light from slits of windows glinted off cheekbones and noses and knuckled hands and, occasionally, a shining eye.

When Mass was over, we walked out together into a swirling mist that had settled over the stone chapel. My kinsmen melted into the mist as though they had never existed.

Behorleguy
France

Cutting ferns
Behorleguy
France

96

*Woman
with scythe
Behorleguy
France*

Behorleguy
France

Madeleine Laffargue
Tardets
France

99

Madeleine and
Pierre Laffargue
Tardets
France

100

Larrau
France

St.-Jean-de-Luz
France

Because it was the first one to come into the valley, there was much shaking of heads when my cousin sold his oxen and bought a tractor.

The wealthiest farmer in the valley even came to remonstrate with him about it. "We can do without that sort of thing around here," he said. But then he stayed to watch the amount of work that a man could do with a machine, and he went out and bought the second tractor.

Soon, I remember thinking then, there will be tractors everywhere in the valley. It is inevitable because progress is inevitable. One cannot resist it. One would be foolish even to argue against it, because he would not have reason on his side.

Still, I thought, how sad it would be to see the oxen go. To trade the warm barn smell of an animal for the unlovely smell of oil. To trade a hand-hewn yoke of polished wood for a steering wheel. To trade the nuzzling touch of a great soft nose for cold, unloving metal. To trade a friend for a machine.

But I knew even then that that was progress. And one would be foolish to argue against it, because he would not have reason on his side.

Above timberline
St.-Jean-Pied-de-Port
France